PASSING
THE
TORCH

Jack Holefelder

PASSING THE TORCH

A business guide to help
small family business owners
pass the torch to the next generation.

ISBN 0-7414-2910-1

Published by:

PUBLISHING.COM

1094 New DeHaven Street, Suite 100
West Conshohocken, PA 19428-2713
Info@buybooksontheweb.com
www.buybooksontheweb.com
Toll-free (877) BUY BOOK
Local Phone (610) 941-9999
Fax (610) 941-9959

Printed in the United States of America

Printed on Recycled Paper

Published January 2006

Table of Contents

Special Dedications

To my mother, who endured all the pains of a growing business and the many hours my father spent to make the business successful; who suffered through all the hard times that go with operating a growing business and then suffered the loss of my father just when times were starting to get better.

Also to my father, who always thought he had the best job in the world and loved every minute of the time spent working with his family. We all miss him very much.

To the first three generations of my family who preceded me and helped me develop the entrepreneurial spirit, the work ethic and the desire to carry on the family tradition.

To my sister, Joan, who will have to make some difficult decisions concerning the future of our family business.

To those family members who work in a family business and who labor through the seven day work weeks, fourteen hour days, family and business stress and who still enjoy the whole crazy situation and wouldn't have it any other way.

And lastly, to the fifth generation of our family business, Diane, John and Sharon Holefelder, who now have their hands on the torch with me. May you be guided by the same work ethic, dedication, vision and luck that your forefathers possessed. The day will come for you to carry the torch alone.

Acknowledgements

I would like to take this opportunity to thank everyone who has encouraged me to complete this book and get it published, through their well meaning nagging every time I came up with a different excuse why it wasn't finished.

To everyone who has offered to transcribe, translate, proof read or rewrite for me, just to get me motivated to get it done.

Especially to my wife, Faith, who has the confidence that I will be successful no matter what I do.

To Kevin McKinney, my life long friend, who has never missed an opportunity to give me a good nature shot for procrastinating on getting the book done.

To my friend, Phil Dyamond, who suggested that I write a book even though by now she probably forgot that she did.

To Dick Davies, John Bogosian, George Luttrell and Jack Gross, who have been mentors and friends and advised and encouraged me throughout my business career.

To Barbara Zippi, who helped get the front cover designed and continually urged me to finish the book.

To Jim McKay, who also helped to design the front cover.

To Dave Smith, for his help with proof reading.

Introduction

Although many of the stories in this book have tragic endings, the purpose of the book is not to highlight the sad endings, but to bring recognition to the fact that these endings could have been prevented if the individuals involved in the businesses had taken the necessary time to plan for the future of the business and for the future of their family members in the business.

There are over ten million small family businesses in this country and eighty percent of them fail to pass on the torch to the next generation. My hope is to preserve a greater number of family businesses by bringing to the attention of all future entrepreneurs, as well as those already in business, the fact that the salvation of the business, the future harmony of the family members and their own peace of mind is in their control. There is no substitute for a well thought out business plan of action, as well as a well thought out plan on how the continuation of the business can be assured.

"Passing the Torch" is based on actual cases of which I have had first hand knowledge or businesses in which I participated in the actual problem solving. The names of the individuals, the locations of the business and the types of businesses have all been fabricated to protect the confidentiality of those who have confided in me over the years. Any similarity to a specific businesses or individual concern is merely coincidental, because the stories you are about to read happen every day all across the country. Hopefully, this book will prevent these disasters and improve the chance for the successful continuation of ownership in your family business

About the Author

I was raised in a family business that spanned three generations. The first generation were entrepreneurs in their own right, working as farmers and repairmen. My great grandmother even had her own milk company in the early 1900's. I followed my father as the president of our family business, who, working along with his uncles, was preceded by his father who generated almost every business idea our family has had since the 1920's.

My grandfather was a man of vision. In the late twenties, he foresaw a great economic boom and encouraged the family to build a community swimming pool. The family went along with the idea and opened it in the spring of 1929. I'm not sure what my grandfather really foresaw, but I do know that he was also lucky because the depression that followed Black Tuesday in October, 1929, while bad for the overall economy, was very good for the swimming pool business. As it turned out, the swimming pool business has a reverse effect to the economy: good economy, bad season, bad economy, good season. Sometimes it pays to be lucky.

I grew up in an atmosphere of seasonal businesses. In addition to the pool, we added a recreational trailer sales business before most people knew what they were. Here again, hard work, combined with vision or luck or perhaps both, were the keys to success. We also sold mobile homes for the mobile home park that sprang up next to the pool. The brothers had guts and the willingness to take the risk involved in starting a business and the willingness to work the long hours to make it successful. Aside from working the family business, they all had jobs working in the local mill. It's still the same formula today that makes successful entrepreneurs in the business world; have a niche in the market and combine it with hard work. Having a little luck thrown in doesn't hurt either!

My father began to take over the business not long after he returned from war in the late forties. As times began to change, my father, although I'm not sure he realized it, had become quite the politician, staying on top of all of the changing regulations and guidelines that began to govern the way business was conducted in our community. His greatest ability was managing people. As he was running the family business, his father and uncles were beginning to retire to Florida and second and third generation children and cousins began to work in the business. He always said the work was easy; the real challenge was keeping all of the relatives happy and working together.

My father expanded the business to a level that would not have been thought possible considering the fact that he developed rheumatoid arthritis of the spinal cord at age twenty-seven. He lived in constant pain until he died at the age of fifty-two. He never once let this malady deter his desire to keep the business going. I remember the days when he would roll off the couch from an after dinner nap and, while on all fours, would breathe very slowly until he could gain enough energy, strength or courage to work his way to a standing position while using the couch or coffee table for support to get on his feet. The pain must have been incredible, but the desire to achieve was even greater. He refused to succumb and to use it for an excuse not to produce. My father was not about to let his illness slow him down, nor was he going to let me get by without working. I remember when I was in my early teens and my dad would come into my room early on Saturday and Sunday mornings. He would pull the covers off the bed and ask me if I was going to be a bum and if not, let's go, we have work to do. I started working at the pool when I was eight and had a weekend job throughout high school at Klines Department Store, which is now the Marple Commons Shopping Center in Pennsylvania.

Some of my father is in me as well. I did the same thing to all of my children and they have always had jobs and have learned how to make a living. A good work ethic is necessary to succeed.

I returned from Vietnam in 1969 and went to work in our family business. My intention was to only stay there about two years until I found something else. However, I ended up staying eight years during which time I gained deep respect for what my relatives had built and a love for the business that I didn't expect would happen.

On November 22, 1976 my father died suddenly and I was thrust into the family business leadership at the age of twenty-nine. The torch was now suddenly placed in my hands. What happened after I accepted the torch of succession was one of the reasons for writing this book.

When I took over the leadership of our family business, I didn't realize how ill prepared I was to deal with all the different personalities that owned the business and the employees that worked in the business. I often thought of my father's words, "the business was easy, keeping the family members happy and working together was the real challenge."

I soon figured out that what you learn in college has little to do with running a successful family business that has several generations of aunts, uncles, cousins, nephews and nieces working in it. Wow! What an education in human nature! I could write several case studies just on some of the situations that took place almost every week. Outsiders always told me that my father was the glue that kept everything in order; how right they were.

Some of the lessons I learned cannot be found in a college textbook. What might seem to be a good business decision to some can be viewed as a bad business decision by a seventy-five year old uncle, especially when that decision was made by a twenty-nine year old. I learned that making long run business decisions was not relative to an eighty-year-old aunt and that interpersonal and interfamily relationships take precedent over logical business decisions. Everyone had their own agenda and the future of the business was not on everyone's agenda.

Because of this lack of knowledge and understanding, the year following my father's death was the most difficult one I have ever experienced. Vietnam had been much easier. I wasn't sure that I would physically survive it. Business wise I did not survive it.

The generation gap, combined with the personal agendas of the senior partners, resulted in months of conflict. One of my uncles worked behind my back to destroy any chance that I had to be successful by uniting the older stockholders against me with trumped up charges to scare them. Every decision that I made was challenged. Even though we were having one of the most successful years in the history of our company, my uncle's campaign of personal destruction was successful and I was fired the week before Christmas, 1977.

What a conclusion to my dream of carrying on the family business. Actually, not really the conclusion, but one hell of an interruption. For the rest of the story, I encourage you to read though to the end. Few people can really appreciate the emotional stress that is connected to being a member of a family business. The stories you will read in "Passing the Torch" are based on fact. They were derived from personal knowledge or direct involvement that I had with other family businesses while acting as an arbitrator, facilitator or just as a friend.

I really feel that a family business, despite all of its potential drawbacks, can be one of the most enjoyable and satisfying times in a person's life. It is hard, but not impossible, to have a successful business. It takes a lot of work, understanding, planning and honesty within the family to make it work. It does not just happen; you have to work hard at it, communicate with all concerned and plan, plan, plan for the future if you intend to pass the torch to the next generation.

Author's Note

You will find that this book is written in very basic language so as to be easily understood and written in short stories with a moral and a lesson to be learned. By taking just a few minutes a day to read one story, you will gain enough valuable information to help put you on a path so that you can pass the torch in your family business.

Buddies Till the End

Two good friends worked at a major corporation in the same engineering department and lived in the same neighborhood. Their wives were best of friends and their children were all about the same age. They enjoyed traveling, camping and fishing. In short, they just enjoyed each other's company.

For years, Ed and Harry had this idea to work for themselves and get away from the corporate stress that they disliked so much. The American dream, to own your own business, was to be theirs. They just knew it would only be a matter of time.

One day, while scanning the papers, they found a sporting goods store advertised for sale. They investigated it and decided this was for them. Since they both enjoyed sports, they felt that this was the answer to their dreams.

Ed and Harry arranged for loans from their parents and the local bank and also took money from their own personal savings to make the down payment needed to acquire the business. Then they both gave notice to the company they worked for and began their new lives as business owners.

They decided that they would make all decisions jointly and that if one partner disagreed with a specific course of action, they would not do it. They both must agree on all decisions. They also decided not to complicate things with any business formalization such as partnership agreements. They would continue with the same handshake agreement they made when they decided to buy the business. A dream come true!

Now you might be saying, that's the way business should be done, without all those legal documents that are time consuming and aggravating. It probably should be how we operate a business, but in today's society, you really can't leave the future to chance. You have to take matters into your own hands. You may not be able to tell what the future will bring, but you sure can have a say in what's going to happen to your business and your estate if something does happen to you. If you don't, the IRS or some judge will.

Let's get back to our case about Ed and Harry who, for years, worked day and night to make their sporting goods business successful. Since they were both trained as engineers, neither one of them had a business background nor grew up in a family business. They soon realized that it wasn't easy to own your own business and they better change the thinking they had developed in their major corporation jobs if they were going to be successful.

They had planned to set a time to talk about the future of their business but never got around to it. Then Harry and his family went on a camping trip and Harry fell and broke his back. Harry was severely injured and was told that there was a possibility that he might never walk again. He would need operations, physical therapy and rest in order to get better.

At first Ed said, "Don't worry Harry, everything will be all right. I'll be able to cover for you." I'm sure he really meant it at the time. His emotions overruled his good business judgment.

Then major problems began to surface which Ed and Harry had never discussed or even thought about because they had never sat down to talk. First, since they both devoted all their time to the business, they never discussed

2

how they would replace the other person if something happened. They figured that if either one of them died, his life insurance would cover his family. They never considered a disability as a reason for the loss of a partner.

As time passed, Ed put more and more hours into the business to keep it successful. Although Ed was able to keep the business running, he neglected his personal family life and this caused contention between him and his wife. It got so bad that she finally gave Ed an ultimatum…either the family or the business. Ed realized that it was impossible to continue at the present pace and save the business and his family relationship. He and Harry made the decision to sell the business. Ed returned to the corporate world. Harry, however, was not able to work again and had no disability insurance to fall back on.

Even the best of relationships should have some form of legal documentation, some plans for disaster and some plans for success. Professional advice is available and should always be gotten to help prevent tragic endings to businesses and friendships.

There are numerous ways to locate good professional help in your community. Most areas have a Chamber of Commerce and local business associations that have referral services. The National Association of Accountants has chapters around the nation and the local bar association can also be helpful. Also, find a qualified financial advisor and an insurance broker. One of the best methods is personal referrals from other successful business owners.

But He Said I Would Be a Partner

In Virginia, Tom owned and operated a small but very successful retail store. Tom had taken over the business from his father and grandfather a number of years before. The business had always been successful and Tom looked ahead to the day his son, hopefully, would take over the business.

A few years later, Tom finally got his wish. After finishing college and taking time to find himself while he traveled around the country, Tom's son decided to join his father in the business. Tom, of course, made him a partner right away. This is what Tom had worked for all his life, to have his son take over the business. It sounds like a happy ending to a nice story and it is for Tom and his son, but not for his son-in-law.

Not long after Tom's son entered the business, his daughter, Mary, who did not work in the business, married one of Tom's best employees. Tom was delighted because he really liked the boy she married and that meant that he would now have two sons in the business. Tom was a family oriented person who just loved the idea of being near his family. Tom was the envy of all of his friends in business. They couldn't believe that he could have such a great business and personal relationship with his son, daughter and son-in-law.

The years passed by and Tom's son-in-law thought that Tom was going to make him a partner in the business. However, that's not what Tom's will said.

A short time later, Tom passed away in his sleep. The will that Tom had was the last one his attorney drew up for him after Tom Jr. joined the business. He had all the proper insurance to take care of his wife and the business. The only problem was that he didn't take the time to update it after his daughter got married.

Although Tom was probably going to make his son-in-law a partner, and most people believed that possibility because it was Tom's nature to do it, the will still read differently.

Not long after his death, Tom's son took full control of the business and decided not to take his brother-in-law or his sister as a partner. Tom's son felt that he had the right to make that decision since it was his father's business and he was already part owner.

After two long years of legal battles with his sister and brother-in-law, which were all won by young Tom, his brother-in-law left the business, taking along with him the family unity that Tom's father had always been proud of.

The bottom line of this story is be sure to take the time to review your will at lease once a year. Times change, people change and so do situations. The best bet is to do a complete review at the time you do your year end closings with your C.P.A. At that time, you are aware of your current values and everything is in the forefront of your mind. Schedule a meeting with your Insurance Agent, Estate Attorney or your Financial Advisor to review the current value of all your insurance policies and personal finances at the same time. Make it part of your yearly obligation to yourself, your business and most of all to your family.

Ask yourself the following questions. Does my will address the needs of the business and the family if I die tomorrow? Will my insurance cover all the gaps that would be created by my absence? Is my business valued properly to assure my heirs will have the ability to continue the business? Have all the tax implications that would occur from my death been covered?

I realize that all of these issues are difficult to sit down and realistically face every year but, if you do, you will have the business continue as you want it to and the peace of mind it will give you on a day-to-day basis is worth every minute of your time.

The Unknown Element

A few years ago someone I know, who was born and raised in a family business similar to mine, decided to stay and work in the business with his relatives. Since his father had died a few years prior to his completing school, his closest relative in the business was his father's brother, Uncle Dave. All the others were cousins and after several years, most had left the business. Joe always felt pretty secure because his father's brother said he would always take care of him and for a while everything went pretty smoothly. Joe never really participated in any of the real business decisions. As a matter of fact, Joe never owned any stock in the company because after his father died, Joe's Uncle Dave purchased his father's shares of stock from Joe's mother.

Joe worked the business very diligently and was a really dedicated employee. When his Uncle Dave died, Joe got the biggest shock of his life. Dave's wife sold the business without consulting anyone, including Joe. She became very bitter after her husband's death and reacted with what appeared to be too much haste. But nonetheless, she did sell it and the new owner soon replaced Joe with someone from his other companies. Joe's years of hard work went down the drain.

As it turned out, Joe accidentally found out from another source that the banker his uncle and father had dealt with all those years had worked out a private deal on his own with the new owner of the business, who turned out to be a friend of the bankers. Soon after Dave's death, he chose the most opportune time to present this proposition to Joe's Aunt. She never thought about Joe or the other employees at the

7

business. It wasn't because she didn't want to, it was just the current state of affairs in her life that weakened her ability to make rational decisions and she agreed to sell the business.

In order to have prevented this disaster, Dave should have had his attorney draw up proper agreements that would have protected Joe. Joe himself should have been wise enough to discuss the subject with his uncle and schedule a specific meeting to discuss the future of the business. Dave's wife shouldn't have been so hasty with her decision, but Dave could have prevented that with the proper planning. Maybe his attorney and accountant urged him to plan but he ignored the inevitable, like many business owners do. Just twelve hours a year could have preserved another family business. Twelve hours out of the entire year dedicated to discussing and planning the future continuation of your business can prevent most disasters.

You Never Know

A few years ago in a little town in western Pennsylvania, I had a friend who was in the recreational vehicle business. We attended the same conventions and trade shows because we sold the same brand of travel trailers. My friend, Kevin, had a very successful dealership which sold over two million dollars worth of trailers every year. He was always the one who won most of the sales awards and vacations from the manufacturers. Kevin was quite a character and his wife, Lois, was just as outgoing when it came to parties and the usual convention revelry. Those two seemed like best friends and perfect partners for this kind of business.

Kevin and Lois shared all of the duties in the business. Lois took responsibility for the paper work, payroll, ordering, dealing with banks and keeping everything organized. Kevin took responsibility for the service shop, sales, deliveries and all maintenance.

Kevin and Lois were in their early thirties with no children and plenty of time to devote to their business. All the ingredients for a successful business and marriage were in place. It wasn't hard to see why they sold so many recreational vehicles. Their energy level was unending. I always made the mistake of trying to keep up with them during the conventions. I only succeeded in wearing myself out.

During one convention in Texas, there was a very noticeable void in the activities. Kevin's name didn't appear on the list of award winners or the vacation group that was going to Mexico, courtesy of the manufacturer. Even more noticeable was Kevin's absence from the convention. I checked around and no one had seen him.

After a day of activities I ran into the manufacturer's representative who serviced both Kevin's business and ours. I asked him what had happened to Kevin and he told me that not long after last year's convention, Kevin's wife, Lois, had filed for divorce. He wasn't sure of the reasons but he did know that all of the energy and desire that Kevin had to succeed was gone. He said Kevin had begun to drink very heavily and every time he stopped to visit them, Kevin or Lois were nowhere to be found. The service manager was generally the one who seemed to be in charge.

With Lois gone and Kevin not in his right frame of mind, the bank began to worry about the large amount of finance charges and the over-extended floor plan that wasn't being taken care of. Customer complaints began to mount and sales dropped drastically.

The nasty divorce battle that ensued for the next year and a half almost destroyed Kevin mentally, physically, and financially. I never discussed with Kevin any of the details of his problems although I did see him when I purchased two of his trailers for customers for whom I couldn't get factory orders. I do know that when Lois left, she not only took half the business with her, but also took the company's organizational skills and the business knowledge necessary to run a successful business. Kevin was lost. To pay off Lois and her half of the business and find someone to replace her took all of the available capital that Kevin had.

I guess it must have been his ego that made him keep the business going when he knew that he was so financially extended that his employees made more money than he did. He went through at least four replacements for Lois in less than one year. The bank finally cut off his line of credit and the manufacturer wouldn't ship any new merchandise unless it was C.O.D.

I saw Kevin about two years later. He was doing very well as the top salesman for a manufacturer of recreational vehicles. He never discussed his divorce from Lois but I did hear his lecture to business owners on the value of partnership agreements. He was very emphatic about formalizing every business with written agreements, whether you are in the business with your wife, brother, son, daughter, father or mother- anybody at all. Learning from your mistakes is the hard way to do things, but they leave an indelible mark that, hopefully, you will never repeat now that you have seen what happened to Kevin.

Never Too Young

A friend of mine from Cincinnati, Ohio had four children, two of whom worked at his golf club. Sam never enjoyed a really good working relationship with any of his children, but it was especially poor with his two younger sons. He always felt that they would never stay with him and when they were in their late twenties, they did leave the family business and started their own commercial janitorial service. Sam knew that a large part of his problems with his sons was his fault because of the way he was. Sam grew up through the depression and, I suspect, he never really recovered from the pain and suffering that he and his family went through. His children never could relate to Sam's philosophy of doing business which was, to say the least, antiquated.

Sam felt that his kids should feel lucky to have a nice job and a place to stay. That, he figured, was all that was necessary to motivate someone. Maybe it should be, but in today's society, younger workers are only looking at today and maybe the weekend. The big decisions are which car to drive, which mall to visit, or which party to attend. Working six or seven days a week in a family business for an embarrassing wage (compared to their friends) is not conducive to keeping younger family members interested in the business.

Well, Sam's two sons got off to a fast start in their new janitorial business. I don't think they ever realized how much they had learned about running a business from their father. I never did, until I left our business. It's nothing you can put your finger on directly, but just the overall attitude and common sense that you learn by working in a small business.

As it turned out, they ended up working harder and longer in their new business than they did working for the old man. As in most new businesses, you have more time and energy than you do money, so they had to take a substantial loan to buy the truck and equipment they needed to handle the larger commercial contracts they were able to secure. I wonder how many contacts actually came about because of Sam's reputation in the community?

After several years, they began to expand so much that they decided to open another office, borrow some more money to buy more equipment and hire some additional help. The two boys seemed to complement one another perfectly. Their business relationship was a good one. A bright future was in the making. Then, one night, tragedy struck.

One of Sam's sons had purchased a new Corvette and on the way home late at night, he crashed into a pole and was killed. Sam was heartbroken and his younger son was left without his business partner. With two offices, trucks and contracts to fill, his youngest son tried to continue the business, but soon found out that his brother's hard work and interest in the business were impossible to replace. He hired a friend of his and made him manager, but that soon ended because his friend's wife didn't appreciate the long hours and weekends he spent at work and not much pay to compensate for it. Young Sam soon realized that he and his brother had extended themselves financially a little too far. The extra money it took to try and fill his brother's place was more than enough to make him fall short of his monthly mortgage payments. He began to sell some of the equipment and closed the other office. He also lost two very big contracts for lack of performance.

With the pressure really on to convert his time into money for mortgage payments, young Sam succumbed to the stress and the pressure and sold the business. He made enough money from the sale to pay off his debt and eventually went back into business with his father.

In short, the moral to this story is that no matter what the age of the entrepreneur and their partners, they should always plan for the unexpected. Before expanding, make sure your base assets are secured. Growth is good, but it should be well planned and prepared for. Every business owner must set aside at least twelve hours a year to review the business with his or her business attorney, accountant financial consultant and insurance representative. Look at it as a yearly physical. If you want to make sure you stay healthy as you get older, make sure you get an annual physical. The same kind of preventative maintenance is necessary for your business too. If Sam's sons had looked ahead and prepared their business properly, young Sam would still be in business today.

She Had Everything

I knew a businessman from Vermont who owned a very successful vacation resort. There was horseback riding and camping during the summer months and a first class ski resort during the winter. It was the kind of place you dream about owning, one hundred acres of outstanding real estate that God had created. It was hard to believe that one person could own such a place.

Mike's big dream was to have his daughter take over the business one day. He sent her to the best boarding schools in New England. He wanted her to have the best of everything: best schools, best clothes, and best cars. She lived the life most of us only dream about- vacations in Europe during the summer and the islands in the winter. Mike spared no expense when it came to taking care of his daughter. He use to take her pictures everywhere with him and was more than a typical bragging father. You could tell she brought him much happiness.

About three years passed and I realized that I had not seen Mike at the annual conventions. Everyone said that the only thing they had heard was that he was having some problems with the business and he didn't have time to attend the conferences. The following spring, Mike came to a regional convention and I couldn't believe it was the same man. He looked sick, worn out and very old. He had also become very quiet and withdrawn. There were no offers to show pictures or do some typical bragging about his daughter. It didn't take a psychologist to figure out that something drastic was wrong.

After several days at the conference, word had circulated around that Mike was looking for a buyer for his business. I couldn't believe it and everyone else who knew Mike and had seen his property in Vermont was stunned.

When asked, he would say that it was time to retire and travel around the world. Then he would end the conversation by just walking away.

The night before the conference was over, I was walking back to my room after dinner when I ran into Mike in the hallway. I asked him if he wanted to stop by my room for a drink. To my surprise, he agreed. We sat for a few minutes just talking about some of the events during the conference. He was very soft-spoken and a little uneasy. I could tell he wanted to say more but I avoided the temptation to pry until he became very quite and tears began to roll down his face. What was to follow was heartbreaking.

Mike went on to explain why he decided to sell his business. His daughter hadn't been home in over three years. She decided to quit her final year of school and live with a beach boy in the Bahamas. For a businessman well respected in the community, he couldn't handle it and almost lost control of himself emotionally and physically. He told me how he had flown to the Bahamas to ask his daughter to come home. She refused and her boy friend put Mike, bodily, out of the house in which they were living. She never even tried to prevent it. The more he spoke, the more he cried.

Mike couldn't figure out what had gone wrong. He admitted that the last few years were not easy ones with his daughter, but he gave her everything she needed and now she turned her back on him. Mike told me he almost decided to kill this guy before he came to his senses and realized he would only make things worse. He made one more trip to the Bahamas to try and convince her to come back home and this time she asked him to leave and never come back again. With that, Mike got up and went back to his room.

I never saw Mike again after that night. He left early the next morning without saying goodbye to anyone. The last I heard, he had decided not to sell the business. However, his daughter still had not returned home.

Mike's story, or at least part of it, is not too uncommon. Many parents give their children too much, thinking that the kids will get all of the things that they never had. This situation many times leads to problems. One of Mike's biggest mistakes, where the business was concerned, was that he never took the time to train someone to help run his business. He never took the time to really train his daughter, even if she would have come into the business. She never really had a feel for it. He had made all his plans in his mind but never sat down and discussed them in a business manner with his daughter. He was too busy giving her all the material things she ever wanted, but neglected to instill in her a sense of values, respect and a solid work ethic.

Back Room Billy

A very successful car dealer, who had learned the business himself "the hard way," decided the best way for his son to learn the business was, of course, "the hard way." Start at the bottom, learn the ropes and teach him a little humility along the way. Good sound advice for a father to give to his son or daughter, right? Well maybe it is, but yet again, maybe it's not. There are always a few problems with that mentality. Some fathers try to pay their children forty-year-old wages and practice forty year old management tactics with them. There usually is a double standard; one for the regular employees and one for the relatives. I believe that owners should lead by example and there should never be special privileges that the other employees are aware of. I'll explain as we progress with this story.

Another problem most business owners have with this old world attitude towards business management is that it usually does not entail a plan of progression for their children. If they are going to learn the business from the bottom up, make sure you have devised a plan that you can discuss with your son or daughter so they know what the future holds. It is good business to discuss such matters with all of your employees, not just your children.

When I have sat with business owners and actually analyzed why their child left, I usually find out that the son or daughter felt left out of the main stream of activities. Business strategy meetings didn't include them. They usually received all the garbage details, the overtime assignments and the lower wages; not much incentive for a young person to want to stay around. Now you might say, if they don't want to pay their dues, they don't deserve it. Paying dues is one thing; outright abuse is another. And don't think the other employees won't take advantage of this situation, especially employees who are in management positions and have their own personal gain in mind. They would love to see the competition for top spots disappear. You can't underestimate the negative influence these employees can have on a young, impressionable family member.

Now, back to the story. Our successful car dealer became even more successful as the years went by and Backroom Billy still worked in the back room as the parts manager after working his way up from lot attendant, garage assistant, assistant parts manager. Five years went by and, during that time, Billy still hasn't learned anything about operating the business. Sure, he knew what parts go in what cars and how to spit shine a show room car and he even learned how to tune up an engine so it purred. Great! He never learned how to run a business, never learned how to manage bankers, lawyers, obstinate employees, promotions, advertising and everything else that a decision maker must do in their own business.

Now we get to the good news and the bad news syndrome. The good news is that our car dealer, although an archaic manager where his son was concerned, did have all his personal planning completed by his professional consultants. His will, his insurance documents and his bookkeeping were in order. When he died a few years ago, there was a neat, clean and orderly transition of ownership. The wife was taken care of handsomely and the son became the new owner of the business. So what's the bad news?

Well! The bad news began when Billy suddenly took over as the new president, the position held by his father for over forty years. Needless to say, Billy wasn't prepared for the challenges of owning his own business. The sales manager seized the opportunity to throw his weight around. Since he had been there over thirty years, he felt that he was entitled to a bigger share of the profits. He had sold most of the cars and was familiar with all of the customers. This created an adversarial relationship right from the start. It didn't last too long because Billy fired him rather than deal with him. The sales manager moved over to a competitive dealership that day. Billy had no previous experience in management and only had his father's business reputation to live on, but bankers like to see results more than past reputations. When the sales manager left and Billy took over his duties, the bank became very nervous and began to put limitations on his financing terms. To try and save money, Billy decided to cut back on his advertising and promotions. Not having the sales experience to understand how devastating the lack of advertising can be, sales potential began to erode.

The service manager could see the change and that business was rapidly decreasing and he left the dealership for a better offer from another competitor. Billy wasn't too upset because he had a friend that was a mechanic so he made him the new service manager. At this point, Billy lost his assistant service manager because he quit when he didn't get that job. To save some additional dollars, Billy decided not to replace the assistant manager. This caused dissension with the other mechanics and the quality of work began to suffer. Customer complaints increased at a rapid rate. With no buffer between himself and the problems of the business, plus the problems of the management procedures concerning the employees, Billy began to drink excessively. I've never seen a problem yet that drinking ever cured. As a matter of fact, it only compounds the problems and will cause health problems which decrease one's ability to perform at an executive level.

Profits began to shrink and Billy wasn't sure why. He didn't have the ability to comprehend the total business concept. With the pressures mounting and problems coming from all directions, Billy had a nervous breakdown.

The last time I saw Billy, he was still recuperating at home and the business was up for sale.

Learning the business from the bottom up is not a bad concept. It can be an excellent foundation to build future leaders from your business. But don't forget to include them as you plan for the future in your meetings and educate them in all the areas of managing the business because, one day, they will need the business skills to carry the torch themselves.

The Remorseful Father

One of the most interesting cases I worked on involved a father who was separated from his children for many years due to a nasty divorce. The father spent most of twenty some years making a new life for himself and became very successful. Then unexpectedly, he had a massive heart attack and almost died. During his long recovery period, he had many long hours to consider his future and think about his past. He felt it was time to have his children around him again, so he did what he thought was right. He bought them each a business. Since he was a successful businessman in his late fifties, he felt that he could help oversee the progress of his son in the newspaper business and his daughter in the restaurant business. Aside from some of the obvious problems you have already thought about, the businesses were six hundred miles apart.

The father is one of the nicest and most ethical businessmen I have ever met. On the other hand, his children are spoiled and unethical. They knew nothing about running a business, never had their own business or even studied business while in the best schools daddy could provide.

The son took a well run newspaper, making a decent profit and well respected in the area, and turned it into an absolute zoo. The town businesses wanted nothing to do with the paper and pulled out their advertising. The son continued to live in high style, continued to buy new cars and travel around while the business collapsed.

The father didn't realize what was going on until it was too late. When he finally fired his son, the paper was hundreds of thousands of dollars in debt with almost no hope of re-establishing its credibility in the community.

Unfortunately for our remorseful father, his daughter turned out to just be as bad as the son. When he purchased the restaurant, he retained the manager's contract from the previous owner because he was the logical candidate to assist his daughter with the business. As it turned out, the manager could see a good thing and started dating the daughter. The two became infatuated with one another and let the business slide. The other employees became disgruntled with the attitude of the manager who became very possessive about the business. The good employees quit and went elsewhere to work. Those who stayed began to steal, profits dropped drastically, morale was nonexistent and customers stayed away. Concerned with his problems with his son's newspaper that was on the rocks, the dad didn't pay much attention to his daughters business until the day he received a letter from his hometown bank informing him that the restaurant would be closed and padlocked by the sheriff.

I figured this would be enough for my friend to have his final heart attack, but he hung in there. First he sold both the businesses and then he paid all the unpaid bills from both businesses. He decided to get remarried and move away, leaving his children a very simple message, "Don't call me! I'll call you!"

This was one of those situations where the remorseful father was destined to be disappointed. However, all of the personal advice in the world would not have changed his decision. Trying to clear ones guilt complex can only lead to more problems if you do not practice good common sense business management.

The Generation Gap

This is a story about a family run hardware distributorship. The father decided the time had come for him to retire and let his four grown sons carry on the family name and family business.

The oldest son was twenty-two years older than the youngest son and nineteen years older than the middle two. They were essentially a generation apart. When the youngest boys were born, the oldest son was already working in the business and doing quite well. Being very hard working and frugal, the father assumed that things would stay status quo and never formally planned the future of the business. Besides, he thought that his oldest son would carry on the tradition and take care of his brothers.

After the father retired and moved to Florida, the oldest son took over as President and CEO. He was the only son to own stock in the business. He became a tyrant where his younger brothers were concerned. He kept the three of them in outside sales and refused to sell them stock. He said they would have to put in more time getting experience. In the meantime, he promoted his best friend to Vice President of Sales and another employee to Vice President of Operations.

When that happened, the two middle sons had had enough and decided to leave the business, much to their father's chagrin. Not only did they leave the business, they went into direct competition with the family business. Another hardware distributor hired the two brothers and paid them substantially more than the older brother was. Since both of the boys had spent all their time in outside sales, they had built up substantial personal relationships with all their clients. The profit picture of the family business began to look very dismal.

However, that wasn't all that would happen to our hero at the top. The youngest son, who also spent all his time in sales, didn't receive any better treatment when his two brothers left, so he found himself a partner from another company and went into direct competition with the family business also. It was not a pleasant picture for our retired father in Florida to think about.

All this aggravation could have been eliminated if our retired dad would have prepared a succession plan that would have protected his younger sons.

Never depend on common sense, good nature or blood to prevail, because when it comes to money, even the most understanding people sometimes have their judgment clouded for one reason or another. Avoid the pain and suffering on everyone's part and plan ahead. If you don't want to make the decisions, get some outside help in the form of an advisory board that will understand your situation and can help you make these important decisions without the emotional family ties.

No Will? There Will Be Problems

A business friend of mine, who lived in New Jersey, was very successful starting and operating businesses. In fact, he was so successful that he became a very rich man. He had one son and one daughter. During his mid years, his wife had died and he remarried soon after. He bought a large estate and moved his new wife into a mansion. On a corner of the property he built some smaller buildings into which his son and daughter moved. Having more room than he anticipated in the smaller buildings, he began to rent rooms. My business friend simply couldn't resist the opportunity to start another business. Everything he touched seemed to spawn another business. Everyone always figured that one day he would own the entire town. And if he were able to keep the pace he had set for himself, he probably would have.

As time progressed, his daughter got married and moved to another state with her husband. His son began his own business and was on his way to becoming modestly successful. Everything was progressing like a storybook of business success stories until my friend began to lose his health. Since he owned and operated every business himself, he didn't have anyone he could depend on to oversee the businesses on a daily basis. He had never encouraged his daughter or his son in their early years. As a matter of fact, he was so cantankerous that he discouraged them to the point that they didn't want anything to do with him or his businesses. His wife didn't have any idea of what business was about, so she was unable to help. He tried to operate from his home, controlling everything by phone. However, his businesses began to slip away faster than his health. The problems were compounded when he had a stroke. One by one the businesses started to close. With no direct management from any authority source, the employees literally stripped away any value what so ever from the businesses.

With back bills due, the suppliers began to stop deliveries. With taxes due, local government agencies padlocked the businesses doors and began proceedings for sheriff sales. If all that wasn't bad enough, some major lawsuits were filed against him and his businesses. It was a shame to see all that he had built start to fall and eventually collapse. But the worst was yet to happen.

You might be wondering how things could possibly get worse but they did. Not for him personally, because he finally died in his sleep one night and ended his suffering. This supposedly smart businessman should have had someone working with him, or had someone groomed to assist him when necessary. He should have had his accountant prepared to help make decisions with him in a time of need and he should at least have had his attorney prepare a detailed will properly explaining the disbursement of his property. He died without a will for which there was no excuse. I wonder if he would have avoided writing his will if he knew what would take place after he died?

His wife, who was his second wife and not the mother of his children, forced the son off the property. This might not have been so bad except that not only did he live there, he operated his business from there. The daughter, who had moved to another state, wanted her share of the estate as soon as possible. At this point, the son, now in need of money to operate his business, joined in the battle. Everyone obtained a lawyer to fight for their cause. Everyone obtained a real estate agent to do a market assessment of the property and everyone obtained the services of an accountant to check the business books. The banks that had given him the

27

business loans were now looking for their money and the back taxes were due. Our Uncle Sam always gets his share, especially when there is no will. What a battle! Sounded like something out of the Mad World Movie or some old horror movie starring Lon Chaney.

Is this any way to run a business? Of course not! As it all turned out, everybody got rich except our business owner's family. Three of his businesses were sold for back taxes and loan balances. One business burned to the ground. It wasn't insured. The estate was carried through the auction process three times before it was finally sold for fifty percent less than its true market value. This whole process took over three years to complete. The administrative costs were astronomical. Everybody, other than the family, was the winner. The family lost just about everything.

You have just read a case in which a businessman totally ignored the principles of good business management and destroyed everything he worked for all his life in just a few short months. Why some businessmen won't take the time to plan for the future always amazes me. In some cases, the business lawyer, accountant, insurance consultants and financial advisor can share a good portion of the blame because of their poor advice. But in this case, knowing the personality of the man and his strong will for doing things his way, I would have to put the burden of blame solely on him. You can't help someone who doesn't want to be helped.

Dying Friendships

About eighteen years ago, two friends of my father went into a machine shop business. Their partnership began when they bought the business they had been working in for a number of years. Jim was the sales manager and the administrative type. Bob was the production manager and very mechanically minded. So it was only natural that they split their duties of ownership in the same manner. Jim remained in the sales end of the business and Bob in the production end.

As the years went by, Bob and Jim brought their sons into the business. The business began to grow. Jim and Bob were well on their way to owning one of the most successful machine shops around. They became so busy that they ignored some of the basic management details that any good business owner should do on a regular basis. They didn't communicate with their professional advisors. You might ask how I knew they didn't communicate with their professional advisors. The next paragraph will give you the answer to that question.

Late one winter night, Jim was killed in a traffic accident. The fate of his son told me that there wasn't any communication on long range planning, estate planning or insurance counseling. Not long after Jim was buried, Bob obtained a loan from the local bank and purchased Jim's stock to pay off Jim's widow. Jim had died without insurance and left a mortgage on the house, which was created when he borrowed money to buy his share of the business. Now, you might say, that didn't work out too badly since Jim's wife got paid off. However, Jim's son had already put eight years into the business as a machinist and had figured that one day he would be an owner of the business. The only thing he didn't plan on was his father dying. The main thing to remember here is that Bob's working relationship and agreements were with Jim, not Jim's son. Within the year after Jim had died, Bob made his son Vice President. Bob took over the sales and administration of the company.

Jim Jr. had offered to buy into the company with Bob and his son, but they refused. Now Jim's son had to face not only the loss of his father but also the rejection and loss of the business his father had worked so hard to help build. He had planned on one day taking over from his father and working with Bob's son. Jim Jr. had dedicated himself to the business. Now he was just another employee.

Jim's son crumbled under the emotional stress the two loses had created and began having health problems. He began to miss more and more time from work. Bob gave him a month's vacation to try and seek some professional help. He didn't do it and his problems only became worse. He developed bleeding ulcers and other symptoms that go along with extreme stress. Six months later, Bob fired Jim's son. He remained on unemployment until he couldn't receive any more benefits. He hasn't worked in almost seven years and lives with his mother who had to go out and get a job to help pay the bills, since the money she received from Jim's share of the business wasn't enough to carry her to retirement.

Not a very pleasant ending for a family that should have had things better, considering the fact they did all of the hard work and experienced the suffering that goes along with building a successful business. It really seems ridiculous when you think that our two businessmen were so busy building the business that they had forgot to plan for the future. All they would have had to set aside would have been about twelve hours a year to sit down and communicate with their professional advisors. Just twelve hours a year dedicated to the future health of the business would have prevented this catastrophe.

Equally Divided-Divided Forever

There was a private club owner from Maryland who called me one day and asked me if I would join him for lunch to discuss some problems he was having with his family owned business. Not being able to resist the opportunity to assist someone and hopefully save another family business, I agreed.

As it turned out, my friend was in the process of making out his will. He thought that he was being fair to his three sons but he still had some doubts because of something he heard me say during a speech a few months before.

He proceeded to tell me that his business was worth a little over one million dollars and was free and clear of any liens. He had decided that his house and his property, plus some stocks and bonds that he and his wife had accumulated over the years, would be sufficient for his wife upon his demise. So he did what he thought was fair; he divided the business in three equal shares between his three sons. I was mortified. I couldn't believe that he would do that after hearing one of my speeches and my constant harping about the unforeseen problems that are caused by the seemingly fair but usually tragic consequence caused by not making good solid business decisions. Let me explain. I asked my friend to give me the current background on his three sons. I already knew, but I wanted to hear it from his lips again. Hopefully, he would remember my speech. I figured that perhaps he was not in the room when I covered that part. I was trying to avoid assessing my impact as a speaker. After all, there was a big cocktail party the night before and he probably had a hangover!

He began to explain that his middle son, Fred, was very involved in the business and had made some new improvements. This gave my friend the time to attend conventions and take some extra time off with his wife. Fred was being groomed to take over the business in a year or two.

His oldest son, Tony, was a fairly successful business-man in his own right and was living across town in a nice home, driving a nice car and was surrounded by all of the trappings that go with a successful business operation.

However, his youngest son, Willie, wasn't sure what he was going to do with his life. He hadn't found himself yet. He was married, unemployed, but his wife had a good job and supplemented his unemployment check.

I could tell by the look on my friends face that he was still satisfied with his decision and no new revelations had come across his mind in the last five minutes. I had to bring him back to reality without making him feel like he had just created the biggest atrocity in a family owned business, which he did. But, I wanted to let him down easy.

My first question to my friend was "Are you aware that there is a strong possibility that after you go to that big business in the sky, your sons may never speak to one another again?" He told me I was crazy and assured me that his sons always got along fine. If you think the Hatfields and McCoys had a feud, you have never seen the ravages of family business fighting. My friend missed one important ingredient and that was taking into consideration the involvement of his sons' wives. Each one was married and very capable of being swayed by a jealous wife.

He asked me to explain. I proceeded to outline a hypothetical problem for him. Number one son is doing just fine and his business is going really well. Suddenly, due to the economy or competition, he needs money to expand, pay bills or take his wife on a trip, which she is used to taking every few months. Where is he going to get the money? He doesn't need to go to the bank because he owns one third of the business. Suppose Willie's wife gets tired of seeing Fred's wife in a brand new car, and a nice new home? By the time she gets done working on Willie, I guarantee that he will be looking for his share of the pie from the business also. Where is Fred going to get all the money? He might even be forced to sell the business to pay them off. I asked him to think of the problems that situation could bring. I've seen it dozens of times. Envy and jealousy became the rule. Brotherly love goes out the window. Blood may be thicker than water, but that green stuff can divided an entire family tree, especially when you have influence from those who married into the family.

There are many ways to be fair to your children by using your best judgment along with the best professional advice you can find. I'm quite sure you will find an equitable solution that will satisfy your desires to be fair and keep peace in the family. Remember, equally divided does not always mean it is fair. Think long and hard if you want to pass the torch in a manner that won't set the business and family on fire.

A very unfortunate event happened one week after our discussion. My friend had a massive heart attack and died. Within two years of his death the business was sold and two of the sons no longer speak to one another. I wish he had heeded my earlier suggestion in regards to revising his will. He did not and their torch went out.

The Jesse James Syndrome

This may seem like a sinister title, but the problems that can be caused by this syndrome ARE sinister in nature, although they are not usually planned that way. Jesse James are usually nice guys, or at least they seem to be nice guys, before either greed and /or opportunity overtake them.

There was a very successful shoe store owner in Pennsylvania who owned three profitable stores. Hal obtained his first store from his father who began the business in the early 1960's. When Hal's father died, he left two thirds of the business to his wife and one third to young Hal and both decided to keep the business going. Hal Junior kept expanding to the point where he was almost ready to open his forth store but then decided to scrap those plans. They were able to maintain the good business standards that Hal and his father before him had set and their business kept doing very well.

Everything went along quite well for a few years. In the meantime, Hal's widow began to date and eventually married an old friend. This didn't change the operation of the business because her new husband had a good job at a large company in town. Everything seemed like it was doing really well, until Hal's widow became very ill and died shortly thereafter. This was a terrible tragedy, but not as much of a tragedy as that which was about to happen to Hal's son.

Hal's widow had never given thought to business arrangements concerning her son. She didn't make any formal arrangements for her shares of the business to pass on to her son. Now there was a new owner; the man who entered the business due to the death of his wife. Now Hal Junior not only had a new owner to contend with, he didn't even know much about him. The animosity began to grow rapidly. His new stepfather decided that he really didn't want any part of the business to begin with so he sold his shares to a major nationwide shoe company for a large sum of money. This left the son to fend for himself as a minority stockholder in a business that had been in the family for almost forty years.

Needless to say, the son was unable to contend with the new owners and their corporate management system. Push came to shove and Hal Junior was given an ultimatum and he sold out to the corporation. Although he did do fairly well on the buyout and managed to move to another part of the state and start a modest shoe store on his own, he still lost the business that his family had built and he did not receive as much for his minority shares as his stepfather (Jesse James) had received for selling his majority ownership to the corporation.

Here again is another example of a total lack of good business management. By failing to use long range planning and projections for the total business outlook, including preparations for continuation of the business ownership, the business was lost. If you are going to bring your children into the business and use their training and developing years to learn how the business operates, give them the opportunity to put those years of training to good use as the future owners of the family business. Make sure by including the necessary provisions in your estate planning for the business. If you want to pass the torch, you need to plan for it to happen.

The Missing Link

This is a short but important story because it highlights the importance of keeping the line of communication open between all of your professional advisors.

The family of a man who owned three very successful flower stores found themselves in a serious bind after the untimely death of the owner. The three stores had been started over twenty years ago. The owner's son and two daughters had been working in the business for several years. The owner had always intended to begin making his transfer of ownership, but for some reason never got around to it. Besides, a few years back, his friend, who was in the insurance business, assured him that the policy he took out would cover any needs his family would have in case of his untimely demise. What his friend never took into consideration, however, was the property values that had increased over the years. He based his insurance on what he thought the market value of his business was at that time. His friend in the insurance business knew how tight he was with his money and proposed a low cost, minimum coverage policy. When Cal died and his property was evaluated for tax purposes, the real estate value of the ground was three times that of the value of the insurance policy. Although the businesses were successful, there wasn't sufficient cash flow available to pay the taxes. The banks decided not to lend them money because they knew the cash flow was not adequate to pay the principle and interest. It became necessary for the children to sell two of the properties just to pay the taxes. After that, a battle ensued over the operation of the one remaining store. Two of the children wanted to maintain the operation and the other wanted out. After a short while, it became necessary to sell the third property to pay off the one child who wanted out of the business.

If Cal had taken the time to discuss his business needs with his accountant, attorney, insurance representative and financial advisor and keep them all informed, his accountant would have recognized the exposure he had with the increased property values and his lawyer may have been able to construct a proper buy sell agreement that had the funding available to protect everyone's interest. Remember, they work for you and you pay them. Make sure you get the best advice from all of your representatives. Have them communicate with each other to make sure you have all of your business assets covered properly.

Threats and Promises

A few years ago, I sat down to talk with a friend who was having some difficulties in his family business. Gary was a fourth generation business owner in his late thirties who had recently suffered the loss of his father. Family businesses can be emotional enough without adding the grief suffered when a parent dies.

The stress he was under resulted from the combination of the business itself, the loss of his father and the pressure being exerted by other family members in the business that were not actively working in the business due to retirement. Unfortunately, they owned a substantial portion of the business and were seizing the opportunity to try and sell the business. This would bring to an end a four-generation family business whose name was synonymous with success.

Gary looked pale and thin. He was working seven days a week, twelve to sixteen hours a day. He was not receiving any support from the other owners because they were fighting to get their own way, which, depending on their position, was either to sell the business or bring in their own children who had never made the commitment to work in the business.

Gary's problems didn't start when his father died. They actually began years before that when the older family members didn't make their commitment to the future. They either resisted or neglected to organize their business matters with professionals who were truly concerned about their client's business. The advice they did receive was ill advised, antiquated and in some instances maybe criminal.

I found out from Gary that the buy/sell agreement that was in force was written by a second generation lawyer who got the business because his father had it before him. He never communicated with the family members or the accountant (which is another story) and left the buy-sell agreement unfunded (no insurance). Another friend, who was the insurance consultant, never investigated this area of the business either. Therefore, after a death in the family, the remaining owners had to come up with the hard cash to buy out the heirs or keep them as partners. Since the sum of money needed to buy out the heirs was too great at the time, they became new partners in the business.

Gary, who was truly committed to the family business tradition, was emotionally and physically losing the internal battle. He had to contend with the pressure of not having control of the business decisions but being responsible for its bottom line. He told me about one particular instance. About eleven o'clock one night, as he was still working in his office, he was visited by one of the owners and was asked to sign an agreement to give a portion of the business over to his kids who never worked in the business. Gary said that after a brief conversation in which Gary declined to sign the paper, his partner became abusive and threatened his employment in the business if Gary did not sign the document. When Gary continued to resist, he was threatened again and this time the partner promised to have him fired and said he would personally do whatever it took to see it happen.

There were numerous maneuvers by his business partners and family members which included calls to his recently widowed mother, telling her that she was going to lose her shares because Gary was out of control and spending too much money. Insinuations were made that he wasn't concerned about his mother's welfare and didn't even call her mom any more. These were flat out underhanded lies. His mom, who was in a vulnerable time in her life, began to question and a major family conflict erupted.

Gary's wife was receiving late night phone calls at home from one of the other stockholders warning her that Gary was out fooling around and not really at work.

All of this got to Gary. He became despondent, lost weight and developed stomach ulcers. The pressure of the business finally took its toll. Gary left the business, never to return.

Here again we have a classic case example of successful business owners taking the future for granted and letting life take care of itself. Unfortunately, this is the strategy that closes family businesses, separates families and causes emotional stress beyond comprehension. All of this happened because the owners were not willing to face the decisions necessary to insure the continuation of the business. Personal agendas took precedent over the continuation of the business. Another torch went out.

Plan Ahead!

Make some notes on this page
for follow up with your advisors.

Conclusion

Now that you have had the opportunity to read some of the disastrous family business stories, I would like to present some suggestions and guidelines that can help preserve your business entity and your family entity. The suggestions are very basic, but very essential for successful family business continuity.

The first, and what I feel is the most important rule, is to remember that your attorney, accountant, insurance representative and financial advisor work for you. They should be interviewed and their references should be checked. You should feel secure that they understand what your business is about, who all your family members are and what your ultimate plans are for the continuation of your business. Managing a small family business can become less confusing and less complicated by applying this basic philosophy and understanding: **your professional advisors work for you, you do not work for them.**

I have found that many small business owners become intimidated by the fact that someone is a lawyer or a C.P.A with degrees hanging all over their walls. The important thing to remember here is that no matter what college or university they attended, you still know more about your overall business and what you want to accomplish more than any lawyer or C.P.A. In fact, just because a person is a lawyer or certified public accountant doesn't mean they know anything about operating a small family business. This misjudgment is more common with small business owners than you would believe.

Finding a lawyer is a very important process and should not be left to chance or be chosen just because ol' Joe was the lawyer for your grandfather, or ol' Bill is a friend of the family, or ol' Mary is a good gal and doesn't charge too much. That type of selection process will most likely lead to poor and inadequate advice. In the long run, it could be more costly and potentially crippling to your business. Your lawyer can be one of your most important advisors and conversely, can be the most destructive if not selected properly.

You must determine that the attorney is qualified to give you advice about legal matters pertaining to your business. What type of law have they specialized in, if any specialization at all? Most importantly, find out what type of business background they have and what other business clients they deal with.

After you have determined that you have found the right attorney, you should set the ground rules for paying their fees. This is a very difficult pill for many small business owners to swallow, because it is very difficult for someone to appreciate the service work of another person, especially when the bulk of the work performed by your attorney will be done when you are not around. The hourly fee you pay can be well worth it in the long run. The money is sometimes hard to rationalize for a small business owner because they don't pay themselves that much money an hour or at least that is how they think. Believe it or not, this is a major problem because the business owner will cut corners or withhold information just to expedite the process and try to save money.

You should agree on fees or on a flat rate basis for handling any particular case or a percentage basis for recovery of a loss. If you are into an hourly agreement do not be surprised by the cost. A lawyer's time is their most important asset and likely to be very expensive so, investigate first. You shouldn't let price alone be your guideline to retaining an attorney. Their experience and reputation could be well worth every cent you pay.

You should also determine how much a phone call would cost. The cost for phone calls varies depending on the individual, the firm or the relationship you have with them. You should also keep in mind the related business costs that your attorney might incur. A few could be secretarial work, postage, travel and other miscellaneous office supplies. All these elements are included in the cost of your legal advice.

Depending on your type of problem or size of business, you might need to discuss retainer fees or contingency fees. Also, depending on the type of arrangements you have with your attorney, you may need to make arrangements to pay their fees on a payment plan basis. Periodic payments are generally acceptable in a long-standing relationship.

For a list of attorneys you can contact your local or state bar association or contact your local Chamber of Commerce. Most will be delighted to provide you with the necessary information to begin your search for a lawyer. And, most importantly, if you don't feel you have the confidence at any level with your lawyer, don't waste time which could cost you your money or your business. Fire him or her and find another one. You may also need more than one attorney, depending on your specialized needs. Remember that they work for you, you don't work for them.

Finding an accountant is almost like finding a lawyer. You should go through the interview process after you determine what type of accountant you need. You may have the need for a certified public accountant or you may want to use a public accountant. The professional requirements for a C.P.A are more rigorous and the need for continued education is necessary to maintain their competence level.

They are also guided by a professional code of ethics that help guide their performance.

You can always check your local Chamber of Commerce or the local accounting association for a list of professionals in your area. The important fact to remember here is that all accountants don't or can't perform the same services. You must be able to determine, through your interview process, what services can and will be provided that match the list of needs you have in your business or on a personal nature. You need to determine what work you need done, such as preparing financial reports, auditing financial statements, preparing tax returns, providing bookkeeping assistance, securing loans or designing an accounting system for your business or personal affairs. You may want continuous advice on financial management and other accounting aspects of your business. This will all be based upon the size and complexity of your business.

According to the American Institute of Certified Public Accountants, some of the questions you need to ask that will help you locate a good accountant are as follows:

- Will your company's financial statements need auditing?

- What services are most important to you; auditing, tax advice or accounting?

- If you manage a company, does it have several installations?

- What are the special requirements for reports to the government?

- Will you need help preparing a business loan application?

- Do you need help with personal financial problems, personal income tax or estate or trust issues?

Don't forget this person will work for you, so make sure that you select someone you not only have confidence in, but also make sure you can work with them. Also, depending on the complexity of your personal situation, there may be a need for your attorney and accountant to work together. Don't keep them in the dark. Make sure they work as a team for you. A failure in communication can cause a lifetime of problems for you and your heirs.

After you have selected your accountant, you need to set the ground rules for their fee structure and how you will pay them. Fees are generally based on time. The level of experience and reputation will be a determining factor in their cost. Here again, don't hire your accountant based on the fact that they don't charge too much or your Uncle Joe uses them or your grandfather used their firm for thirty years. Your needs are unique to you and your desires are different from your friends or your family. Keep your priorities straight and get the best accountant you can work with.

The best way to get the most out of your accountant, according to the American Institute of Certified Public Accountants, is to talk over all of your plans and objectives with your accountant. If they are to give you advice on your investments, taxes and financial management, they must know what your goals are. Let them know exactly what you want and need from their services. Keep good records. This will cut down on research time if your accountant has to look for them. Anytime you make a change in your personal or business direction, make sure you inform your accountant. Ask them for ideas and suggestions that can help you make certain decisions on investments or decisions on the management of your business.

If you don't feel that you have the confidence in your accountant or that you are not receiving the service or advice you have expected, don't waste time; fire them and find another accountant.

Finding your insurance professional and financial advisor can be just as important as finding your accountant or your attorney. Their advice is necessary to protect your business and your family in the event that you reach your retirement goal or if you become sick or disabled. You need to discuss the plans you made with your accountant and your attorney. If you have a partner, a wife or children that you would like to pass your business on to, "Passing The Torch" becomes much easier if you have prepared for every contingency of business continuity. Over eighty percent of family owned businesses fail to pass on the business to the next generation. Many times that reason is a failure to provide the money to buy out partners or pay taxes or pay off other heirs who may not want to stay in the business. Your insurance plan can provide for these contingencies.

Your insurance professional and financial advisor need to meet the same ethical and professional standards you require from your accountant and your attorney. Confidentiality is a must. Their knowledge and understanding of your business and personal needs is a must and your ability to work with them as a team is a must. They must have knowledge of insurance programs and special business related plans that will enhance your prospects for a successful transition to your heirs or partners. There are literally hundreds of insurance agents and financial advisors to choose from. Your attorney or accountant will recommend one if you ask them to, but no matter how you locate one, make sure you go through the interview process to insure that you found the one you can work with. Keep in mind that the commissions they earn from the sale of insurance programs you purchase usually compensate them. This makes trust and confidence a must and the need for a team dialogue with your attorney and accountant very important in order to avoid unnecessary or excessive insurance coverage or, worse yet, not having the proper coverage.

If you feel that you are not receiving the advice or service you expected, don't waste time; fire them and find another one.

If you follow the previous suggestions on hiring your professional advisors, your prospects of "Passing the Torch" will be greatly increased. What I find in most of the cases that I become involved with is that procrastination runs rampant. Most business owners are usually working six to seven days a week and say they are too busy to take the time right now. Many say, "I'll get to it soon, I know I should have it done." Unfortunately, many of these "should haves" have failed in their desire to pass their business on to the next generation.

To help avoid this procrastination, **sit down now and look at your schedule**. I'm sure you will find some time open in the next few months to schedule an appointment with your professional advisors. Mark the date and block out the time in advance. Long range planning should always be a part of your overall business plan. Decide now that you will spend at least twelve hours over the next year with your professional advisors. Budget your time and budget your expense. The long-term results will assure your peace of mind, that your family will be taken care of and your business will continue in the family name. You can pass the torch but you must **plan to make it happen**.

They who hesitate will lose.

Summary

It is much easier to sit here and write down all of the things it takes to insure your success as a business owner so that you can pass the torch to your heirs, than it is to actually organize your time to get it done. However, those who do take the time have a higher degree of success than those eighty percent that do not get to pass the torch.

No business is easy to manage in today's society and managing a family as well makes it even more difficult, because, many times, the emotions of a family business override the necessity for timely management decisions. When the business problems are discussed in the boardroom as well as in the kitchen at moms on Sunday afternoon, you can be sure that procrastination will raise its notorious head.

The conflicts and confusion that arise on a regular basis, due to the various personalities that encompass a family business, make decision making a very difficult process. The owners of a family business who have the intestinal fortitude to make the hard business decisions, combined with the ability to balance all the personalities, will be the successful ones who will pass the torch.

Don't put off till tomorrow what you should do today.

Did you know?

Did you know that there are over ten million family businesses in this country? These small businesses, many of which are run by kitchen table CEO's, employ half the people who work in this nation. According to the Small Business Administration, they generate 43% of the gross national product and during one ten year period created 67% of the nation's new jobs.

Small business is a big business in this country. Small businesses also generate most of the new ideas and inventions that keep our economy growing. One of the main reasons that I wrote this book is to help keep the backbone of our economy, which are small and family businesses, successful.

Eighty percent of all new businesses fail within the first five years. Many of the tips in this book will help small businesses be successful and prepare to pass the torch.

The average life span of a successful family business is twenty-five years. Only 20% of those successful family businesses pass the torch on to the next generation. Of those family run businesses that do get passed on to the second generation, most fail within five years of the owner's death.

Nearly 70% of all business owners do not have a business succession plan. More than half of all business owners do not have insurance to cover personal losses for themselves.

"This is the only chance you will ever have on the earth with this exciting adventure called Life. So why not plan it and try to live it as richly as possible?

- Dale Carnegie

Some Do's and Don't's for "Passing the Torch"

Don't procrastinate. Begin now so you won't be caught without a succession plan.

Don't surmise that just because someone is an attorney, it means they know about business plans, especially yours.

Don't use an accountant just because your grandfather used the same one.

Don't ignore the next generation. Talk with them and train them to be competent managers.

Don't avoid preparing job descriptions for each member of the family.

Don't underestimate the influence of a son-in-law or daughter-in-law. They have their own priorities.

Don't under estimate the influence of your wife or your partner's wife. They have their own agendas.

Don't overlook your own personal development plans.

Don't discourage open communication between family members and key employees.

Don't under estimate the value of your time.

Don't avoid written policies that outline family authority and responsibilities in the business.

Don't be unrealistic when setting your goals and objectives.

Don't forget to plan for the replacement of key business employees other than yourself.

Do have frequent meetings with your family and other employees to discuss the goals of the business.

Do you want to pass the torch? Don't procrastinate! Plan Now!

Do personal evaluations of your children or other family members that are in the business to determine their strengths and weaknesses.

Do some research on your professional advisors and interview them before they are hired.

Do insist on continuous training to develop the business skills of your heirs.

Do you have key personal insurance in case of an untimely loss?

Do you have adequate health benefits for all employees?

Do a periodic review of the goods and services you offer with other family members in the business.

Do an organizational chart.

Do proper documentation of all agreements, written or verbal, that you make with other family members.

The Basic Management Check List

Set goals and objectives.

Have written policies.

Check the reality of your goals with others.

Is your present record keeping system a realistic picture of your business?

Seek legal and financial advice on major transactions.

Make plans for succession in case you die suddenly.

Review your products and services with the intent of improving them.

Make an organizational chart.

Have job descriptions for your key personnel.

Ask outside advisors for their opinions.

Have plans for motivating your employees.

Communicate with your employees and your family.

Know when and where to find assistance when you need it.

Note: Two organizations that can be helpful with your planning and professional development needs are the United

States Small Business Administration and your local Chamber of Commerce.

Each one has local and regional offices that can assist you or point you in the right direction. You can find them in your local directories or online by using the keywords, "small business administration or chamber of commerce."

Resources for Your Assistance

The United States Small Business Administration has its main office in Washington D.C. They also have regional offices around the country. They can assist with financing and management questions.

Your local Chamber of Commerce is listed in most directories. The Chamber can assist with business start up programs, family business councils and local references for professional services.

The local bar association and the National Association of Accountants will be listed in your local directories and will act as a reference for legal and accounting professionals.

Insurance companies are listed in your local directories. Most will give you free quotes and suggestions for different types of coverage that you may need. I have found that references from other business owners are a great way to start looking for a company and a personal representative who acts as a broker for numerous insurance companies. You can also check out the American Council of Life Insurers or the American Risk and Insurance Association,

For a financial planner, you can check out the National Association of Certified Financial Planners which has both state and local branches. Financial consultants can also be located by researching the national brokerage firms who have local offices or small independent firms who can be referred to you by your accountant or other business associates.

HBI Consulting is my personal consulting business firm. For questions or references you can contact me by phone at:

(610) 494-4035

via email at:

jackholefelder@comcast.net

by regular mail at:

Jack Holefelder
HBI Consulting
1000 Park Avenue
Media, PA 19063

Top 10 Estate Planning Suggestions

1. Prepare a will with your legal professional.

2. Be aware of all federal and state estate taxes. Your accounting professional should be your guide here.

3. Prepare your retirement plan with your professional advisors.

4. Make sure that all of your assets are titled to avoid probate.

5. Make use of the gifting laws to avoid some taxes.

6. Choose an executor that you can trust.

7. Keep personal track of all your assets.

8. Do not forget to have cash available to pay taxes. Your banking professional, along with the assistance of your accountant can help with this.

9. Look into creating a trust to protect your assets from increasing your estate tax liability.

10. **Make your appointments today to discuss your estate questions with your professional advisors.**

Make yourself a promise to set your first appointment to discuss "Passing Your Torch."

Conclusion to the Author's Story

After getting fired just before Christmas, with no prospect of finding a job during the holiday season combined with the shock of suddenly not being part of the family business, I had to find inner strength immediately. It was extremely depressing. However, with two sick children and no money to buy food for the family, I had to look forward and I began the New Year looking for a job.

A friend of the family came to visit me early in the New Year and offered me an opportunity to work at his insurance company. That became the first step on my road to starting a new career outside of the family business.

Over the next several years, I had several jobs that helped me get back on my feet. The entrepreneurial spirit and work ethic that was instilled in me took over. I did what ever it took to become successful outside the family business and also maintain my stock ownership in the business.

Over that period of time I continued my relationship with several mentors that I had befriended while I was working at the family business. They were all family business owners themselves. Their continued support, encouragement and advice were major keys in my successful business career that was to follow.

They advised me to hold on to my shares of the family business and eventually, along with my mother's shares of the business, we became the majority stockholders.

Nineteen years later (but who's counting) I became the President, CEO and Chairman of the Board of our family business. We are now in the fifth generation and my son and oldest daughter are now working in the business. My youngest daughter is one of our legal advisors. Is this a great ending to another potentially tragic ending to a family business? Well, the final chapter will still need to be written after I see if we can survive another buy out of another minority stockholder.

The big mistake that was made in our business by the previous generation was not funding our buy-sell agreement with insurance. It is a very well written document and, after 35 years, is still in vogue today. However, there was not enough cash to pay off the heirs of our former stockholders who had passed away. Therefore, they received the stock and we were stuck with owners that had married into the family, had never worked in the business and did not have the same concern for the future of the business.

I am committed to two things: to give my best effort to overcome the financial stress of another buyout so we can prepare for the sixth generation and to keep telling our story to other family business owners so that they can avoid tragic endings and can pass the torch.

**"No One Plans To Fail,
They Just Fail To Plan."**

NOTES

**Why wait?
Do it now!**